FTER DENVER

FTER DENVER

POEMS & PROSE

ADVANCE READING COPY

G BRUISER DOPE BOY

CONTENTS

For Joey, Dave, Jim, and Diane

For my loyal Denver boys

For my mother and father

And, of course, for Patrick, my first real boyfriend

"There is a fine line between liberated and dead inside."

—Joey Russo

POEMS

DENVER

DADDY STATE OF MIND

Daddy is a state of mind
You can hate it, but don't lie
You may think I'm not old enough
But I'm not Chasin' the same things as you

Your eyes make it hard to tell what you're looking for
The Right Eye doesn't know what the Left Eye is doing
Boy, you need some Tender Loving Care
And you won't find it in Kansas City

You can be a kept man
Your daddy keeping you like the secret he used to keep
Or you can go to Whore Boot Camp
Get every shade of dishonorable discharge

You can be like me, kinky for loving the ungrateful
The daddiest trait of all
I've raised enough children today
I'm a Grandfather now—I'll spoil them

When someone tells you they feel lucky
You're then in a situation where luck is involved
All good luck eventually becomes bad luck with Time
So you might end up falling in love with loss itself

Death is what a Western Fool runs backwards toward
Remembering a future that never arrives
I'm a Silver Daddy ready to dismount into the Carnival of Ashes
When I pass through, nobody will be able to call me back

Men twice my age have called me daddy
But in truth, I'm nobody's daddy but my own
I've been my own daddy since my daddy left
Each morning when I wake, I think of what I have to do

Does being responsible mean blaming yourself for everything you do?
How do you know which things to blame yourself for?
How do you know what your intentions are?
Other than notice what's on your mind, what else is there to do?

These are the four questions I ask my daddy (myself) today
And because I'm a good father
A great father with Time
I know to not answer them

When I fall in love with you, I fall in love with you forever
Your favorite person is the person who leaves you alone
I want to call him, but I can't
I'm his daddy, but I just can't call him

AFTER

DENVER, COLORADO

Gay men in Denver, Colorado

Gay men living in Denver, Colorado

Gay men living in Denver, Colorado, who made it their second home

Gay men living in Denver, Colorado, who made it their second home, having sex with each other

I was a gay man living in Denver, Colorado

I made it my second home, having sex with other gay men

Having sex with other gay men was my second home

Doing drugs and having sex with other gay men was my second home

I was living there

In Denver, Colorado

I did a lot of dishonest things in Denver, Colorado

I didn't answer calls from my mom, because I was working

I was busy working in Denver, Colorado

When I wasn't working, I was not alone most of the time

I was scared by my own behavior in my second home

I lied to my first ex-boyfriend about what I was doing in my second home

My second home, Denver, Colorado

I learned from the best in my second home, Denver, Colorado

I drank coffee every morning in Denver, Colorado

I strung gay men along in Denver, Colorado

In my second home, I was a serial dater

I was surviving, but I wasn't living, said my best friend in Denver, Colorado

My best friend in my second home

I didn't have a first home in Denver, Colorado

I ate at Carl's Jr.

Qdoba

Chick-fil-A

Taco Bell

Taco de Mexico

Gladys Taco Tent

The Vending Machine at Trade

The Vending Machine at The R&R Lounge

Benny's

Racine's

Patxi's

Pete's Kitchen

Tom's Diner

Denver Diner

Sam's No. 3

Black Sky Brewing

Burger King

Chop Shop Casual Urban Eatery

Popeyes Chicken

Pepper Asian Bistro

Lechuga's

Santiago's

The French Press

Pudge Bros. Pizza

Blue Pan Pizza

Pizza and Grill

Bourbon Grill, that was my favorite

I would get the Bourbon Chicken with sides of Mac and Cheese and
Cajun Potatoes

My second ex-boyfriend's cocaine dealer was his friend

My second ex-boyfriend's cocaine dealer/friend drove himself to the
hospital in Denver, Colorado

My second ex-boyfriend's cocaine dealer/friend drove himself to the
hospital and had a heart attack

He had heart, lung, and kidney failure

He was put in a medically induced coma

This was over Christmas

When he was missing, I saw my second ex-boyfriend at the bar with
his friends

They were worried

They were partying at the bar

This was in Denver, Colorado

I no longer live in Denver, Colorado

CUSTOMER

His name was Bob

He lived in an apartment diagonally across the street from the bar

He started coming in when I worked, seemed harmless enough

Mentioned he had a husband of forty years

He was a semi-retired consultant in his late 60s

He made a lot of money and traveled for work

He would usually come in within an hour after I opened the bar,
    when there were very few or no other customers

He would pay for two scotch and sodas at once, $7, and tip $3

Sometimes he would tip $5

Bob became interested in my life

He asked me what I did

I told him I was a writer

He wanted to buy my book

I gave him the link to my book and he ordered it while sitting at the
    bar

He friend requested me on Facebook and messaged me

"Please accept my friend request"

I accepted his friend request

He started messaging me on Facebook

He liked about a dozen of my posts in a row

The posts promoted my shifts at the bar, so customers could know
    when I was working

I went to New Orleans to read at a hotel

Bob got my book in the mail and messaged me on Facebook
He was out of town
He brought my book with him
"I'm amazed by your poetry"
"I hope that picture in the back of the book is you"
I told him the naked picture in the back of the book was me, that
     my ex-boyfriend took it when I was pissing and I didn't know he
     took it, then sent it to me a few days later
"You are so sexily handsome to me"
I told him I was glad he enjoyed my work
"I'm headed back to Denver"
"I'm on the plane telling the flight attendants about your book"
"How did the reading go?"
"Did you read '150 Dollars'?"
I told him the reading went well, that I did read that poem
The poem was about masturbating into a jockstrap and selling it to a
     guy while working at a bar

I got back to Denver and resumed work at the bar
On one of my first days back, Bob came in
He brought his copy of my book and wanted me to sign it, so I did
He grinned
"Are any of your poems autobiographical?"
You could hear the inside of his lips peel off his teeth before he talked
I told him I sometimes wrote from experience

On a day off, I went with my roommate to the bar to pick up payroll
My roommate wanted to practice doing tarot readings on customers
Bob was there

She gave him a reading

When she and I left, Bob gave me a hug

"I love you"

I told him I loved him, too

I attempted to terminate the hug

He wrenched my face toward his and kissed me on the lips

This is something Bob had started doing, telling me he loved me and
    kissing me on the lips when he said goodbye

Back at home, my roommate told me Bob's tarot reading was "really
    dark"

He told her he was unfaithful to his husband for forty years, and he
    recently got busted and had to change his ways

He asked her if she read my book

She told him she did

He asked her if she liked it

She told him she did

"No, what poems specifically?"

"Did you like '150 Dollars'?"

"I like to think his work is autobiographical"

She told me he requested to follow her private account on Instagram,
    and she blocked him

I told her he came in with his husband on a Sunday, the only time
    that had happened, and his husband made a joke about him
    being an alcoholic

I told her Bob once made a joke to me about poisoning his husband

A few days later, I was working and my friend Cody was there,
    drinking

So was Bob

Cody and I were talking about Twitter, showing each other stuff we
found funny

When Bob motioned to leave, I didn't come around the bar to give
him a hug

I told him to take care

He looked sad

Later that day, after work, I noticed Bob followed me on Twitter

I looked at his profile

He hadn't been active on Twitter for years

Until now

He started liking my tweets

Replying to my tweets

Messaging me on Twitter, quoting my tweets to me

He messaged me his phone number

"Share your number please"

I shared my number

I tweeted "Getting balls-deep in the tarot"

He replied "Show us"

I replied "Nope"

He messaged me "Ok was just teasing anyway"

At some point during this, my friend Jim told me Bob messaged him
on Facebook

"Are you friends with B?"

He told him we were indeed friends

"I think he's just marvelous"

A few days later, I got a text from a number I didn't recognize

It was a picture of my coworker Chad—my "work husband"—in a
    funny hat

I texted "I love you" thinking it was Chad

The unknown number texted "I love you, too"

The unknown number texted a picture of Bob on a sofa, cuddling
    with a cat

I realized I wasn't texting with Chad

I texted "Oh sorry I thought you were someone else"

Bob texted "Oh haha"

A few days later, I was working at the bar

You'll never guess who came in . . .

It was Bob!

My favorite customer!

I was getting so lonely!

He told me he had just bought four more copies of my book

He told me they were for his friends

They were going to Puerto Vallarta for his birthday

They were all going to read my book

A little book club

"Wow, thank you so much"

"Thank you for your patronage to the arts"

"I really appreciate it"

About a week after that, I was working at the bar

Bob came in

Bob Frank

Robert Frank

My not-so-secret admirer, who lived diagonally across the street from
    the bar in an apartment with his husband and cat

He told me the books had shipped

"So you should be getting those royalties soon"

I thanked him for his patronage to the arts

He told me he was going to write a couple paragraphs about each of
    his four friends, telling me about their lives

Then, based on what he wrote about them, I was to write a personal
    note for each of them in the books

"You don't have to sign them as yourself"

"You can use your pen name"

I started laughing

I was nervous—I'll admit it

It seemed like Bob wasn't the greatest with "boundaries"

I told him no

He protested

"Why not?"

I shook my head

"But I want my friends to know I know the author"

I told him he could tell them that

I told him that was something he was doing for himself

"No way, Bob"

"There's no way I'm going to do that"

I turned and wiped down a reach-in cooler, something I had already
    done twice since Bob came in

He gestured with his hand, shooing the air, and stormed out, his first
    of two scotch and sodas he had already paid and tipped for left
    on the bar, 80% full

Bob . . .

I messaged Bob on Facebook

"There seems to have been a misunderstanding"

I catalogued to him what he had done

I told him it made me feel uncomfortable

I told him what he needed to do if he wanted to continue coming
    into the bar when I was working

"I will never come in again"

"You are so full of yourself it's preposterous"

"Barack Obama wrote me a personalized message in his book"

"As did Tony Bennett"

"Joan Rivers (rest her soul) did so as well"

"Who do you think you are to talk to me the way you did today?"

I blocked him on Facebook and Twitter

I blocked his phone number

Later that week, I was working on a Saturday

I didn't usually work Saturdays

Bob opened the door of the bar, saw I was working, and left

That's right, motherfucker

Yeah, you creepy, pushy bitch

Turn around, Bob

You can drink at home with your cat now

I'm not working for you for free so you can get cool points with your
    vacation friends

I bet they're dreading spending time with you in "PV"

I'm not a politician

I'm not a lounge singer

I'm not a stand-up comedian (rest her soul)

I'm not working for your vote
I'm not working for your applause
I'm not working for your laughter
I'm a writer
I don't make a lot of money
But my life is full
My life is beautiful
I work for nearly nothing so rich, smarmy, scotch-swilling faggots like
    you can pretend to have emotional lives
Here's a new poem
I wrote it today
I wrote it just for you
It goes:
No
No
No
No
No

I'm glad you enjoyed my book, though
Thank you for your patronage to the arts
Hope you have fun in Mexico
Tell your friends

GAY POET HERE

Gay poet here, I write poetry and have sex with people of the same gender

Gay poet here, I write poetry about having sex with people of the same gender

Gay poet here, I have poetry and write sex with genders of the same people

Gay poet here, I sex gender and about people with poetry of the have write

Gay poet here, I people about and poetry havings with sex of the write same

Gay poet here, I same sex with the poetry gender and about people

Gay poet here, I gender poetry with sex workers while shutting my dick in a vault

Gay poet here, I have I about I-ing I with eyes of the I I

Here poet gay, I hate people and the feeling is mutually assured consent

People people people, people people people people people people people

Anal sex dad, Jesus masturbated to the futures of getting ass-martyred by a gay lion

Aye aye aye boy, fuck the poetry shut

Poetry identity politics, dramaaaaaaaaaaaaaaa

Here, I'm gay, and the ass leech has left the non-existent page

Militant mom gone, memory mooch metastasize

Short tall good bad, up down accident purpose

Starred Kirkus review here, my life is an unbroken creek of moral grey areas

Shade: thrown; butt: fucked; vengeance: exacted

Stop reading this right now here, I stop reading this right now and stop reading this right now with stop reading this right now of stop reading this right now

Fake twitter feud promotional tactic dead-eyed bored wannabe blue-collar dad jokes

Gay poet here, I murder the edge of the universe to nobody the
moment for sleep

AHEM

Excuse me, but what are you talking about?

Shut up.

Can you please not do that anymore?

Seriously, stop.

Do it for yourself.

Nobody wants to hear you.

Not even you.

I can feel the outrageous effort of your pain so perfectly it hurts.

I can tell you hate it as you do it.

You probably hate it most of all.

That's why you keep doing it, further and further cursing any would-be recovery from it.

You can't want something you don't deserve, and then get mad when you don't get it.

It's your fault for wanting it to begin with.

Think about it.

Why would you even want that?

Can you locate any foundation of your complaint?

Do you actually think you deserve anything?

Well, if nobody has told you yet.

If you haven't figured it out.

You don't deserve anything.

You certainly don't deserve this, but I'm feeling generous today.

A feeling, like any, that will pass.

You're lucky I care about you.

This isn't "tough love."

It's actual kindness.

You're just so used to your orgy of discouraging niceties that it seems
cruel and unnecessary.

Look.

I wish I didn't have to be the one doing this.

But somebody has to, because nobody else is.

My task here is grim and unsung.

It's like draining a portable toilet into a clown car, wedging a rock on the gas pedal, and letting it drive into a lake.

If you could just for a moment tear yourself away from feeling slighted by an abstraction you created to excuse your unearned attitude.

If you could just pay attention to what I'm saying.

Lord knows you've been demanding everybody else's attention for longer.

It's my turn to talk to you.

Mine.

I am the pigeon that shits in your mimosa.

I am the mutt who lifts his leg on the lies you pad around your life.

I am the friend you didn't know you had.

Here I am, friend.

A trinket in your palm.

You have my attention.

Go ahead.

Say your nothing.

Kick your legs that refuse to stand on their own.

Throw yourself down and scream it into your plush pillow.

I am your pillow.

You're getting me wet.

Please don't get me wet anymore.

I'm wet enough on my own.

I bet you're so pissed off right now.

If you think I'm talking to you, I am.

If you don't, I'm not.

I am.

I'm not.

You can act like it doesn't matter to you.

But it should.

It will.

Don't fight it.

You can't fight time.

Yours has come.

YOUR FIRST EX-BOYFRIEND

I'm going to be your first ex-boyfriend
Most of your friends will become my friends
They will come to like me more than you

I'm going to be your first ex-boyfriend
You will try to keep tabs on me
But I'm not an internet browser, babe

You're an internet browser
You can rent a boy, you can rent a friend
But you can't rent a boyfriend—not really

I'm going to be your first ex-boyfriend
I'm going to make you feel wrong and dirty
But not in the way you like

The way you liked it when I berated you
Like a loving yet abusive father
We get hard for our pasts, as they harden in us

And hard as we try, we all smell like something
I smell like your first ex-boyfriend
I masturbated to you in the shower this morning

It was great, it was mine, because you weren't really there
You were never really there, were you, for me?

I remember what that feels like

I have a first ex-boyfriend, too
He wasn't perfect, but he was better than you
At least my first ex-boyfriend tried

Remember, after it went down (again)
When you said "I'm not perfect, either"?
Perfection isn't what I wanted

I wanted you to try, instead of trying me on, like shoes in the mail
I can only say "I'm sorry" for the same thing so many times
I can only say "I love you" so many times before you'll never know it

You thought, you felt, you thought you felt . . .
You thought you were falling in love, not tripping over mine
I thought your thoughts held the truth

I should learn to pay more attention
I should see my mom more often
I should do a lot of things more often

You should do a lot of things less
It might be time for you to log off for good
And log in to your heart's wilderness

A place scarier than any real place
Is love a real place? I'm trying to find it
I've been there before, I gave you my map

But it's a conquest done on one's own
I'm going to be your first real X
You will be my last fake one

GRIEF FANTASY

I've been having this recurring fantasy/daydream

It's both of my ex-boyfriends meeting for the first time

At my funeral

My second ex has forgiven me for all the harsh, cruel, judgmental things I said to him after he broke up with me, knowing that I was in a lot of pain, a lot of which he directly caused me

My second ex is sad, but he's not fully crying

My first ex is losing it, sobbing really hard, wailing and whimpering, which is very painful right now for me to imagine

My first ex has forgiven me for not being completely truthful with him at times, at other times outright lying to him, or lying to myself in front of him, because I didn't want to hurt him

I was afraid of hurting him

He is crying like he cried to me on the phone when he realized I chose my second ex over getting back together with him, the first person I ever really loved squeaking in a way that penetrates me and makes me think "I'm a bad person" / "I hate my life" / "I want to kill myself"

They meet each other

They know who the other must be immediately

They say hello

My second ex is the first one that says hello and my first ex isn't really into interacting with him

My first ex told me he would imagine meeting my second ex and stabbing him in the throat with a broken bottle, killing him for taking me from him

Even though I chose my second ex over getting back with my first ex

My first ex loved/loves me so much that he blamed my second ex for something that I was responsible for

Because the pain of recognizing it was my fault was too much for him

That last line hurt to write

They start talking about me, and my first ex is resistant, because he wants to just be with his pain and not have to think about me with my second ex, but he eventually breaks down further

He realizes that even though my second ex really hurt me, he's not a bad person, and that if I fell in love with him, that means I must have seen something in him, and that he cared for me

They hug each other and cry

My mom isn't there

They are the only ones there

It's not a funeral

I don't know what it is

It's a forgiveness fantasy

They forgive me and trust that the ghost of me loves them and never wanted to hurt either of them

In the forgiveness fantasy, I can't forgive them, because I'm neither a ghost nor a spirit

I'm not watching them

I'm just dead

I've been fantasizing as if the only way my exes can forgive me is if I'm dead

As if that will force their hands to let go

I didn't commit suicide in the daydream

It was something else—something sudden and tragic

They leave the funeral that isn't a funeral and get drinks

They even laugh together, telling stories about how I was a lovable
idiot

Writing that last line felt good

They say they will keep in touch, because having a relationship
connects them to me

They become friends

I don't want to die before either of them die

I never want this to happen

I'm going to try to not die

I'm going to live as if they will someday forgive me

PROSE

BEFORE
DENVER

SLAB

Some asses were built by the devil just to haunt you. Aoudad, named after the Barbary sheep that roamed his oil-wealthy family's vast ranch along with a gallery of other exotic imported game they'd hunt, was keeper of the fundamental rump that left an indelible dent from whose negative slant of flesh I'd choose my future fucks. It wasn't long after I met him, and it might have been before or even at the same time we were introduced, that I saw Aoudad's bare soft divided push of orbs jiggle solid and pale in front of a locker row's glossy red grates still tacky from the multimillion dollar renovation his father funded for the school's football program, himself a former pro turned petroleum lord who had framed movie posters signed by celebrities in his mansion in the hills behind gates with the neighborhood name on them—an obscene degree of memorabilia shelved and locked on display behind sliding plate glass with signs that all had the same illustration on them of a hand holding a revolver pointed at its viewer that read: ain't nothing I got is worth your life.

No, it was all worth much more than my life, I'd think during team dinners hosted there, even though what the sign meant was if I took anything he'd shoot me, that none of his macho pop culture relics were as valuable as the life I'd lose for stealing one of them, a pair of gloves signed by the famous actor who wore them in the movie about a boxer, to name one. I routinely purloined cash from a box of end-of-day register till envelopes on a shelf high in the bathroom in the back of the pool chemical store where I worked, but I wouldn't dare swipe these tokens of a dominant life. Aoudad's butt was a shelf on which rested a priceless collectible, an object of infinite agony I'd die for even thinking about tickling past the fluid screen of his loving family, his rich daddy's guns. To reach the part of his body I wanted most, I would have to dig an underground tunnel, come crumbling up through the Sicilian tiles in his kitchen's bountiful pantry, pad by his father's private museum of opulent bro-kitsch, past the various rooms with sole purposes—the video game room, the pool table room—up the tall stairs, down the long hall, into his room, where there the plump bulk of it lay, its hard outline faintly perceptible in the dark like my own thief shape. I would have to dig a different manner of tunnel. I began to orbit him online.

The advent of social media coincided with my finding masturbation as one finds religion. I enacted the sequestered fervor devoutly, hourly upon myself, often with encouragement from the computer, though casual scenes from the locker room had already seized my imagination with ample carnal vibrancy to sustain my efforts. Even boys I presumed straight I saw glimpse Aoudad's prize while he changed and showered—it was that grade of marvel, an exceptional chunk of anatomy at which the butchest would gasp. I anticipated and planned my assward glances during those brief windows when the buoy surfaced in full from underneath the fabric, a sun hovering above—squeezed by to bulge—an elastic horizon, the red mesh shorts we all wore. It granted me the eyes of a cannibal. Aoudad must've known, been self-conscious of, its vulgar magnetism.

He was a year below me in school but we were the same age. I was young for a sophomore and he was old for a freshman when he first entered the JV locker room the spring off-season of that year. The coaches were preparing him along with other precocious freshman to play on varsity his sophomore year. He was the youngest of four brothers who'd all played football at East River, some of them going on to play in college, so he was a legacy there, the road already paved before him. I wouldn't make varsity until my senior year, which was standard, the status you earned after two years of pretending for the varsity team to be the opposing team they'd play that week, a duty called "scout team" where you "gave them a good look" of what they were to expect. During the period of the spring of my sophomore year to the spring of my junior year, I had very little contact with Aoudad, only speaking with him for reasons I'd half-fabricated, like asking to borrow his cell phone while waiting for rides in the parking lot after practice. I didn't have a cell phone, yes, but I didn't have to borrow his. I just watched him. It wasn't until the spring off-season of my junior year that we had no choice but to interact, being teammates and in the same locker room again.

Spring training involved a lot of lifting in the new weight room, of which Aoudad's father, Deets Ballast, paid for a large portion. Aoudad and I played different positions—he, a back, and I, a lineman—so I never got to spot him as he lifted, which was for the best, because had I stood behind him as he squatted, which in silhouette was some odd and rigid pantomime of sodomy, I suspect I would've either collapsed or burst from lust. Coach G, the defensive coordinator, told the team at the outset of spring training that he'd be selecting groups of us to travel to and compete in powerlifting meets on weekends. We all had to do it once and, as if to test my resilience in the face of a perfect temptation, one that could decode my longing to the point of total organ prostration, Aoudad and I were put in a group together.

Aoudad seemed gay—it should be mentioned—to myself and others. The matter of his appetite was a prominent murmur. His personality and behavior made a penchant for men all but undeniable. He had a high, bright voice and made pals with girls, mauling and pawing them non-sexually and sisterlike in the common area in conspicuous view of puzzled boys. His backside formed a mound on which his backpack sat. The glut of musclefat protruded twofold from his spine's end near-perpendicularly. The boys he hung around with also seemed to present as gay, if unknowingly, or immutably. I had no idea what they were up to among themselves, maybe nothing of imminent interest to me. I hadn't heard much of anything from anybody other than the most basic-headed speculation that even a stranger such as I had already made. I moved in circles outside the primary ones if not wholly on my own. I wasn't known for being a potential fag. I was known for being a weird person, a spaz, prone to outbursts, wild, crazed, hilarious at times, irritating at others, relentless, defective, puckish, moody, but not gay. Being bizarre was an armor, a camouflage, a diversion that, to me, just felt like living. That secret was nestled safely inside me like a slick, blind, baby eel.

But it's not as simple as not telling anybody you're gay. The "closet," a phenomenal term unfortunately suitable in its domesticity, is a behavioral structure, a carefulness that prevents acting on unlearned desires. It's something anybody can try to be inside of and anybody can try to assemble around anybody else. The closet is pretense. It's not exclusive to sex. Its functional scope is as wide and varied as desire itself. Anybody can live, or be demanded to live by cultural necessity, pressure, or coercion, dishonestly. In a dishonest and hostile world, practical survival isn't always an honest occupation. Often, it's a flat out fraudulent racket. There are gay people who are out of gay closets, yet still confined to others. Some never have a chance to be in the closet, innately deprived of the option of that special lie, ripped from any inkling or scheme of one and punched young. Some feel, and rightly so given their thorny circumstances, that at least part-time concealment is the only maintainable choice. To live honestly in any given moment means to face whatever may thrash from the punitive power of the fearful, confounded, bureaucratic, surveilled and self-surveilling masses. This, however, is not a "coming out" story I'm telling you, a person who is no longer here, so that's all I'll say about that.

SLAB II

At dawn on Saturday, our powerlifting group arrived at the locker room to try on singlets. We laughed because none of us had worn such things before—tight-fitting elastic blue numbers with thin shoulder straps that meandered low and showed our chests and backs. Slipped in one, Aoudad's form became pure abstract with real blood behind it at the same time—ham in shrink-wrap. It's hard to explain a bad, bad want, a vain groan no one can hear.

His friend since middle school, Mike M, a tall blond wide receiver who'd gotten his braces off recently and was a terrifying idea of a person-to-be, came with and from the start they were aloofly buddied-off. You got the sense it was them two and then the lesser rest of us.

"Anybody bring honey?" Coach G said.

"Yeah," Aoudad said.

"Ballast! Is it the bear?"

Aoudad pulled a plastic cartoon bear-shaped container of honey from his bag.

Coach G laughed in a performance of fraternal satisfaction. "Freakin' awesome."

Coach G was an indefinitely extended version of a "super senior." He went to East River fifteen years ago, played football and won all-state honors both offense and defense. He attended college where he daydreamed of blitzes still, married a lawyer woman, moved back to a neighborhood like Aoudad's, became a coach. You could see him as both player and coach in the large team pictures that lined the hall outside the locker room, eyes squinting over a big jaw.

It had been said to us in the week preceding the powerlifting meet, during which it was made sure that our group was executing the various lifts with proper form, that a longtime custom at these meets, one at least as old as Coach G's time, was for the competitor to, in the moments before his lift, swallow a shot of honey. This was to spike his blood sugar and provide him with a surge of combustible energy.

Coach G had said he would enjoy if someone not only brought honey to the meet, but especially if it came in a bear. This seemed like an important point of humor for Coach G. Aoudad delivered.

Transportation was a full-size yellow school bus with a couple dozen rows of brown vinyl bench seats, larger than it had to be for the few of us traveling to a facility in a more rural area. Coach G drove the bus like all coaches except the head coach were trained and required to. Our group sat in diffuse arrangement from just behind Coach G to the very back. I sat in front of Jorge, a guy I'd known and played football with since middle school but with who I hadn't really bonded or become friends. He was the person on this trip I knew best, though, with who I'd spent the most time on busses to and from athletic engagements, so we stuck together like Aoudad and Mike M, who sat next to each other across the aisle from us. I had my own seat like everybody did, lengthwise and stretched out, back against the side wall, head against the window, feet and calves hanging off the inside edge into the aisle. It was doubtful any of us wanted to be spending a weekend morning like this. It seemed Coach G was the only one of us who cared about powerlifting beyond the obligation of the affair, and he wasn't even doing it. Bench press, squat, deadlift, power clean, one ridiculous strain after another, tugs and grunts provoking bloated postures of heroic exertion. I harbored kinetics of a naked order behind the shared tedium of our semi-inescapable situation. We were deep in hill country now, the evaporating remainder of dew on roadside combinations of bluebonnets, paintbrushes, and wild grasses sparkling in a plane of flux. I slid my window down and hurt my eyes watching it.

We traversed the unfamiliar school's multipurpose gymnasium. Mats were spread across the floor and vertically condensable dark lacquered bleachers had been drawn from the walls for teams to sit and rest between their turns in the contest, which was already underway. This locker room was dank and rusted. We quickly switched into our strongmen suits. Once clad, Aoudad and Mike M giggled and took pictures of each other with their phones, fracturing an atom of erotic hatred in my brain. They posed and made intimately silly faces for the lens. Aoudad arched his back in display. How funny and grand it was to them, the extent of his proud component. A pig-colored balloon God inflated. I could've chomped a hole in a cheek right then, climbed inside and died.

We returned to the gym and took our places in the bleachers. It was almost time for deadlift.

"Now might be a good time to break out the bear, Ballast," Coach G said.

Football coaches called players by their surnames, in excess, even if there was nobody else they could possibly be talking to, as a way of applying control. It smacked of militarism. You are named therefore you are had by me. The repetition insisted on this relationship.

The bear appeared and was passed around. Its lid was opened. Its clear body was inverted and pinched. Its sap was let into mouths.

We moved towards the deadlift mats. There were rounds where everyone had to lift the same weight, increasingly, until there was no one left. We all made it through the first and second rounds in our respective weight categories. Aoudad and Mike M were one category down from Jorge and I.

Before the third round of lift attempts, I walked over to Aoudad, leaned my head back and opened my mouth. He knew what this meant. I kept eye contact with him as he squirted in a golden portion.

"Good luck," he said.

I swallowed. "Now you."

He seemed to hesitate, but once I smiled, assuring him of the good-natured reciprocity of the exchange, he braced to receive the gift of substance. My grip got excited and I gave him more than his due of the saccharine deposit, the bear's black dot eyes never rattling from their hermetic trance. Aoudad gagged.

"Too much," he said.

"Sorry," I said, still smiling, "good luck."

I failed at my attempt. The honey could only invigorate the musculature that was already there. I went over to watch Aoudad with Coach G. The heave and clench made Aoudad dark red, almost purple, with a lattice of veins fattening around his face and neck.

Coach G smiled with his mouth open and held his hands above his head. "Yes, Ballast! Yes, Ballast! Yes, Ballast!"

Back in the bleachers, Aoudad and Mike M were giggling about something again. It was a girl with a giant ass. Given the nature of her attire, the whole border of its volume was presented. Though our group was exclusively male, this was a powerlifting meet for both boys and girls. Aoudad furtively took a picture of it with his phone. Coach G told him to quit it.

"Y'all could be related," I said.

Coach G contained his laughter. Aoudad blushed. He knew I was right. He knew they were ass cousins.

Back on the bus, there was a sense of relief that it was over. Aoudad and I were actually having a conversation. The hierarchy had been leveled, if temporarily, by this common experience. I asked him questions.

"Why do you play football?"

"I like it."

"You do?"

"Yeah, why?"

"You don't seem like you do. Do you believe in God?"

"Yes."

"Do you believe in gay marriage?"

He paused. "That doesn't really affect me."

What did he think, that saying he either did or didn't believe in gay marriage would've given him away, so he'd instead better abolish himself from the premise altogether? If I'd then had the nerve and wit I do today, I could've said, "So you're a career bachelor?" He knew I knew he was lying. He lied anyway. There's only so much recognition the constituents of a moment can bear if the fallout of that recognition virtually dooms them. He lied—poorly so—but he wasn't wrong. Gay marriage didn't really affect him. It didn't really affect me, either. It still doesn't, but I have a feeling it affects him now.

SLAB III

I was a glutton all summer, tangled in the lurch of a grudge, driven to the revenge of feeling something not yet felt, a feeling I anticipated and simulated that, upon integrating the warped regime of its memory, would mend the resentment of not feeling it. I wanted to sink my face into Aoudad's haunches like one of those padded rings at the head of the massage tables in the training room, to lap at the winking center of their grainy meadow, to taste past him, polish the floor through his taint with my tongue, plumb for undiscovered metals in a hidden mine, be the hook in the cum-mottled wall on which his taxidermal trunk was mounted. Fucking without complete spite wouldn't be fucking. It would be a righteous deceit. With controlled abhorrence is how you make a boy let you into him. You acknowledge the devastation he is, and he thanks you, because he feels that more than what he's been told about himself in his life so far. Until you ravage him with your blessing, engorge him with your disgust.

This summer, I wouldn't be feeling something not yet felt, at least not libidinally, circling again and again through the rote framework of my yearning. I wouldn't internalize any healing experience, some liberating sexual catharsis where the usual guile of social life would come unglued, but instead would nurse in seclusion a festering device. There would be no spelunking for a seismic hell in the dark meat of a real man, only the invented but nevertheless compelling facsimile, the phonily pioneered-in-fantasy counterpart of what I wanted but couldn't bring myself to endeavor feeling, pushed deeper and more frozen into my desire, cemented there squirming. This was the summer I became a pothead.

In addition to the money I made working at the pool chemical store, I funded my loafing with the money I stole from the pool chemical store.

One weekend I was over at my mom's ex and his wife's place. He'd bought me a bong for my birthday and let me keep it there, in his workshop. He headed project construction for a design-build commercial and residential contractor. He and I were smoking from the bong in his workshop in the late afternoon after I'd helped him jackhammer and remove a broken up bed of concrete from a room in his house he was renovating. The smoke we coughed morphed among the hanging tools and stacked equipment. His wife came in and took a hit.

"I think I need a nap," she said, "it always makes me so tired."

We were more hungry than tired from being stoned. I was giddy with exhaustion and slaphappy. We walked down his street to a fast casual Mexican restaurant and ate burritos, big ones we picked the ingredients for out of steaming and refrigerated metal bins along the counter as the employee compiled and rolled them to our specifications. I chewed just enough to swallow what I bit so I could bite again, to then swallow that bite, bite what I would then swallow of the tortilla silo filled with meat, beans, rice, cheese, salsa, lettuce, etc. I was still hungry, so we went next door to a fast casual Chinese food restaurant. K humored me, paid for my three-entree plate, shook his head watching me red-lidded and shamelessly push it in my face, a yawning trashcan. Yet I was still, if not hungry, desirous to continue eating as a pleasure unto itself, enjoyment derived from the very mechanics of it, so we went back to the fast casual Mexican restaurant and I ate another burrito.

"You can buy this one, boy-o."

I sucked it down like I was proving something to K and myself about myself, testing my capacity. There was an immense amount of pressure in my midsection now, which I clutched staggering back to K's place. I entered his workshop, this time alone, to get high. I took a big hit and coughed, pounded my foot and hooted raspingly, sat and stared at a nail gun recumbent on an air compressor in the corner. I saw Aoudad in my mind, his ass, in the locker room, the group showers naked, slick with hot spray, and in the commons covered by designer jeans with stitching on the back pockets. The unattainable vision throbbed its primal ware, transformed its look and texture, stretched its proximity as if responding to my attention. A bilious gloom surged forward in my abdomen and collided with a hollowness, roiled from the jolt. I fell to my knees and puked on the workshop floor, widely splattering the overeaten food. Breathing hard and sweating a lot, I cleared my scorched and corroded nostrils of the fragments that got diverted to my nasal cavity during the roaring evacuation. I wiped my slack lips on the shoulder of my shirt.

Through the glass in the workshop door I saw K's wife, up from her nap, approaching. She paused on the other side of the glass and I saw her mouth go "whoa." She came in and asked if I was alright.

"Yeah, I took too big a hit. I'm gonna clean this up."

"There's so much of it."

She was kind about it. I forgot my embarrassment as fast as I mopped. I felt better, empty, very high. I was looking forward to when I'd be alone later and could imagine what I wanted to repeatedly at length.

SLAB IV/V/VI

I wasn't ready for two-a-days. That's a practice in the morning and another practice in the afternoon with a break in the middle to eat lunch and avoid the sun. Two-a-days started two weeks before and lasted until the school year started. The go-getters on the team trained over the summer, lifted weights and ran. I ate mint chocolate chip ice cream and jerked off. I was not a go-getter. The world was gradually teaching me a cumulative argument of what I was not, moving me into a place called "not knowing," where I would disappear and things would be noticed.

I can't go any further without telling you about instant messenger. I'd found Aoudad's screen name listed on his social media account back during my junior year and began what I understand now as harassing him innocently enough in superficial pursuit of a friendship with him. Friendship wasn't quite the business I pictured, but it was the language I knew, the method by which I tried to access a language I didn't know. What I wanted was a mystery. It was a mystery to me that I wanted what I wanted, and what I wanted was mysterious and unfamiliar to me, but I also wanted mystery itself. Mystery was what I was after. It's what you're after, too, at this moment, both gone and here with me at the same time. Me, gone and here with you, gone and here with me. There was the world and there was the world. There was the world subject to the world, working to make the world to which it was subject, subject to it.

I was 100% the initiator of all correspondence. It wasn't that I didn't have shame, but shame can be displaced and hidden by desperation's swill. The contents of our conversations were general—just my light badgering of him that only ever extracted small talk designed to end fast—not memorable, except for one time, that was memorable.

I remember it well.

It started like any other conversation: I started it. *Wutangsword88* messaged *ABallast32*, and *ABallast32* messaged *Wutangsword88* back.

"hey aou"

"heyy [X]"

The normal vacuous banter. But then, after things strayed into a different kind of territory, perhaps from my nudging, he asked me.

"do you wanna jack off with me?"

What led up to this, whether the transition was abrupt or smooth, I cannot recall with conviction. The gods of wasted youth, or maybe just waste, have it in their custody now. I might have asked him, straight-up and without preamble, if he was gay. He would've said no. But—he asked me.

"what? are you serious?" I said.

"yeah, it's not a big deal"

"but you said you weren't gay"

"i'm not, it's just a fun thing to do"

"I'm not gay"

"i know, me neither. it's just fun. you just jack off in front of each other and seeing the other person makes you excited"

"really?"

"yes"

"but where?"

"we can do it in the back of my car. i have an [SUV]"

"just park somewhere?"

"yeah after school"

He was a ginger, a redhead. A cup of white yogurt with flakes of dried blood in it. He'd sunburn easily so he had to wear a certain shirt to protect his sensitive skin during practice, on top of all the sunscreen. I was shocked and going insane it felt like. What a proposition. What a . . . trap? Was he setting me up for some public humiliation? I'd seen enough teen movies to have my suspicions.

"I don't want to do that"

I knew he knew I was lying. I lied anyway. The risk leveraged the mystery. I spooked myself. He abandoned the idea and it wasn't brought up again, except for when I brought it up.

Our rapport did change, though. I'd gotten frustrated with him growing a bit cagey after that and one night I ended up copying, pasting, and posting the entire text of his collaborative "rooting each other on" self-pleasuring pitch in the claustrophobic quarters on social media. I messaged him and let him know I did it.

"oh my god please delete it"

"why?"

"please just delete it"

"you asked me to do it though"

I toyed with him awhile, then deleted it. I don't think anyone saw it. I held the power, and then I let go of the power. It felt too cruel. But that power. It felt like a threat on my life.

V

Trouble came in ways of which I couldn't be blamed for being unaware.

I'd done two-a-days before the start of my freshman, sophomore, and junior years and each time got easier because: I got used to how bad it sucked a little more each time; the younger the players, the more the coaches tortured them with up-downs and wind sprints; I went through puberty and became more athletic. So this time around, with my place on the varsity roster secured by default, earned through my years of commitment and dedication to the team, I did nothing to prepare for two-a-days. Any senior could sign up for football—even if he'd never played for the team before, or ever before in his life—and he'd have a guaranteed spot on varsity. After three years of tolerating my voluntary disciplining for social reasons beyond me, my position in this red and blue world of supplemental fathers and birds that ran as fast as cars was the same as someone with none. Freshman, JV-B, JV-A, and Varsity. Pull down the stairs to the attic, retrieve the toys long in storage, play with the toys all night in wonder, and watch your best friend's dad whip him on his bare ass with a belt. You have earned your place.

I was pretty sure I wouldn't start this year. The offensive lineman who played my position in front of me had started last year as a junior after the guy in front of him's heart stopped during the second game of the year, a road game, just keeled over off the bench, the biggest player on the roster with a full-ride scholarship to a Division I school. He was resuscitated with an AED by a dad who happened to be a cardiologist, coming down from the stands to administer the automated current, clearing the body so nobody else would get shocked.

But everybody in the stadium got shocked. Both teams agreed to discontinue play. The guy ended up getting a pacemaker installed for a chronic arrhythmia and wouldn't play again. T-shirts were made proclaiming that now, it was for him. They were doing it for him now! Before, there were a disparate multitude of reasons why they had been doing it, but now, there was but one. The guy in front of me this year rose to fill the team's urgent need and started the rest of the year. Roused by their fallen comrade's spirit in tow, the team went all the way to the state championship game on a miraculous playoff run in which the entire community seemed to invest their souls. Then they lost. Salvation was avoided.

VI

I showed up to two-a-days out of shape. I wouldn't be starting so I didn't see much to be in shape for. Water breaks were mandatory so nobody got too dehydrated. We were told what hue our pee should be: apple juice, keep chugging, lemonade, better, clear, best. Late summer afternoon heat was the enemy. I'd witnessed minor versions of heatstroke in other players through the years but never in myself except for precursory symptoms. It wasn't like it used to be, players whose dads had played said. They said when players in their dads' day got dehydrated or heat exhausted, the coaches would put them in a room without light and have them eat salt tablets and drink water until the cramping, shivering, and dizziness subsided. Our training staff had tanks of water with several spigot hoses running from them. The water break whistles would blow and you'd shamble to the tank, your head cooking murkily inside your helmet, which you'd pull off by prying the ear pads apart and tilting it back so the pads would slide up the sides of your face, drink as much as you could without getting sick, douse your head to cool it off, spray the inner pads of your helmet to get the sweat and grease out. When you put your helmet back on, a nasty chill would wash over you.

The first practice wasn't in full pads—just helmets, shirts, shorts, and turf shoes. The field was artificial turf with a visible ridge halving the field end zone to end zone and gray metal grates surrounding for drainage. The field reminded me of the top of my skull, the crown itself also ridged end zone to end zone due to a narrow birth passage. But my head would flood. There was nowhere for it to drain. I waited for my face to leak and founder. The texture of the field was like rubber sandpaper—coarse and grippy, springy yet stiff with not a lot of give. If you slid and your skin made contact, it got ripped off and left enduring scabs. The field was a thriving Petri dish of staph bacteria. Skid wounds would frequently get infected, skin gnarled with red nodes pregnant with seeping pus. Maybe my brain had a staph infection, flooding its white knots from inside, out of nowhere, out of the hole that was me.

SLAB VII

I'd begun breaching the subject of my anality during this time. Aside from the occasional peeled vegetable, my main utensil was a toy maraca no longer than a marker with a blue bulb and black handle.

During the second week of two-a-days, when by then I'd been conditioned to them enough to indulge in the off time, I pushed the maraca up too far in an especially adventurous session and it got swallowed and lost inside me. The round bottom of the handle slipped past the seal and I couldn't get a hold of its polymer surface with my greasy fingers—only brush the end. I tried to push it out like I would a stool, but the shape of it was such that it kept involuntarily getting pulled back in. I felt the grit shaking as I walked to the bathroom. I couldn't shit it out on the toilet either. I had to get to practice. I left for campus with it still inside.

Coach L, the offensive line coach, had us doing a drill that focused on keeping our feet moving during pass protection. We each partnered up with another lineman and took turns being the pass rusher. The idea was, if you moved your feet quickly enough while keeping a low center of gravity, it was harder to get around or bull rush through your blocking.

"Move your feet, [X]!"

My partner shoved me onto my back.

"Damn it, [X], what'd I just say?! Get low and move your feet or he's gonna put you on roller skates like that every time. Let's reset and go again."

Coach L blew his whistle.

"Chop those feet!"

The maraca's sand jiggled in rhythm. Coach L's command worked—I was doing a better job holding off the pass rush.

I heard the whistle again.

"The hell is that noise? What's goin' on—is one of y'all bein' funny?"

The linemen looked at one another in merry perplexity and I joined them. My sphincter fastened. The maraca rose through my guts to my throat, then floated above my head like a siren of sin. Coach L grabbed the collar of my shoulder pads and pulled me toward him.

"What the fuck is this, [X]?" He snatched the levitating icon.

"It's a maraca, sir."

"A what-ka? How'd it get out here? You tryin' out for jazz ensemble?"

"No sir—I was using it to stimulate my prostate."

He released his grip on my collar, took a step back.

"Ah, uh—well, [X], that's very resourceful of you."

He put the maraca's bulb in his mouth and started sucking on it. He ruminated awhile, twirling the handle between his thumb and forefinger, the bulb rotating in his cheek.

"You know, [X], I've never seen a guy your size move like you. Way I see it, there's no reason you shouldn't be dominating whoever you line up across from. Every play you gotta chop your feet like that."

"Yessir."

He yanked the maraca from his mouth while tensing his lips in a circle, making a wet popping sound.

"You're gettin' enough fiber I see." He winked.

The water break whistles blew.

Coach L slapped my buttock. The maraca shook. "Attaboy, [X]."

As I jogged to the tank, the maraca continued to shake.

THE GIBSON DAMNATION
RESURFACES

I woke early morning on a continent of urine spreading to the edges of my in-laws' mattress. The piss, an acrid, whiskey-laden discharge that was unmistakably mine, had encroached upon my husband's side of the bed, dampening the areas of his skin that touched the flood released in sleep. The soak felt fresh and not yet tepid. The sheets peeled off my back as I crab-walked out of the brass California King frame, sloped crookedly onto the floor and into the lament of the present. He was innocent to the predicament, my little love buoy, anchored and bobbing unconsciously in a puddle of my blunder, his sweet, limp face for not much longer protected from the sourness of his—our—sopping world. I crawled around the foot of the bed, got on one knee like I was proposing to him this time, shook his arm.

"Peter—Peter wake up—I wet the fucking bed. I'm so sorry."

He snorted and rolled onto his back, making the linens squish.

"Hunnhn—"

"I got drunk and peed all over us, baby."

"What?"

Flipping over, he began to appreciate and fear his place of rest until he was alert and bewildered, frozen in a position like he was about to do pushups. He skittered laterally out of bed and stood beside me.

"We have to strip the sheets."

This was the first measure of an until now dormant routine for me. I spent my childhood under the iron gargoyle of this condition, hunched in office chairs while my parents had urological dialogues with specialists. Strategies were exhausted on my problem. I secured detector pads into the crotches of my underwear, snapped awake to a small alarm clipped to the sleeve of my nightshirt, sampled a motley of nose sprays and homeopathic remedies, drank from a jug of filtered water with prescribed minerals dissolved in it, expanded my bladder capacity, eased the struggle of keeping it in. Sleepovers, sleepaway camps, any overnight visitation outside the zone of my persistently soiled den was a waking hazard racked with anxious preparation and snookered by the unforgiving oblivion of dreams.

This was a new ordeal for Peter, though, who, after he helped remove the affected bedding and pillowcases and showered, initiated a plan to clean it all without his parents, who we were visiting for the winter holiday, finding out. Their bedroom was across the house from ours, but Peter said the washing machine, even though it was located adjacent to us, was too loud and would wake his nosy southern mother.

"There's a laundromat down the street. I'll go with you and get everything going, then you can wait there and switch it over to the dryers while I come back here and take care of—" he held his palms upward and pointed his hands down at the yellow abomination, "—this."

There weren't plastic sheets on this bed like the ones I grew up with, so my secretion accessed a moderate circle—the creeping perimeter of which was darker than the center—of the mattress. I imparted my technique to Peter of richly spraying the beleaguered region with an odor eliminator and aiming a hair dryer at it.

"I'm gonna shower before we go," I said. "I don't want to sit there smelling like piss."

The car stunk with the stained fabrics bunched in the backseat. We could smell it well now that we were clean. Peter drove, a cigarette drooping from his lips as he dodged a long pothole in the road.

"Don't look at me like that. I deserve a carton for this."

"I'm sorry, baby. Have as many as you want."

"You told me this hadn't happened since you were a teenager."

"It hasn't. I don't know what happened. I guess I drank too much too close to bedtime."

"Too close to bedtime!"

There was no telling the cause of the nocturnal leak. The best explanation I ever got was it was hereditary. My grandmother and uncle had it, too, a fact I remember my mother soothing me with, giving the humiliation of my youth a membership. I discovered this about my cousin as well one summer after noticing the sleeping bag he brought to camp reeked like mine, disclosing to him our lineage's common woe. Welcome, Cameron, to the private alliance of Gibson pissers.

It was just Peter and I in the laundromat except for an old woman who didn't look up from her folding. We split the load, shoving the duvet cover and pillowcases in one machine and the sheets and mattress pad in another.

"Text me when it's dry and I'll come get you."

He left before I could thank him. I sat and watched the bulk infused with my flaw flop behind the pair of submarine-like windows—two more eyes rolling at my situation. The old woman delicately pinched the shoulder seams of a blouse and laid it on a stack of garments in her hamper. I imagined myself decades in the future as an old lady in a laundromat doing the daily washing of my pissy sheets. A calm swamped my sense of incontinence.

The drying phase stretched on due to the density of the items and my elderly role model departed. I texted Peter.

"How's it going? Almost done here."

"Same. I think I burned the mattress a bit."

"No you didn't. It's supposed to smell like that."

He picked me up. I held the warm pile in my lap.

"Wow, this feels really good. Very relaxing. It's kind of making me have to pee."

I saw him try not to smile, then give up.

Peter distracted his mother with details of the coming afternoon while I snuck in through the garage with the bundle. Rejoined in our room, I hugged him like a blanket I'd ruined and cleansed dozens of times. We turned the mattress over and remade the bed.

AFTER

MEETING

I got home from work at the bar and found a letter from my dad. It was the wrong address, but close enough to make its way to me. I had not seen him in over eleven years, not since I was a senior in high school. In the letter, he told me he hoped the letter found me well. He told me he was going to be in Denver. I lived in Denver. He told me my step-sister lived in Denver, and he, my step-mom, and two other step-sisters would be visiting her. She was getting married. Actually, she was supposed to be getting married, but no longer was, and they were all still coming.

The bar was not a bar yet. It was a construction site. I had been working there six days a week, purging, cleaning, painting, building, whatever they wanted me to do to help it become the bar they wanted. I got fired from my last job at a bar for calling out a few hours before my shift. I was having a panic attack and felt like I could not do it. My former boss texted me that we were done.

I found one of my step-sisters' email addresses on the internet and asked her what my dad's phone number was. I called him and left a voicemail. The next day, working at the bar, I noticed my dad had called and left a voicemail. I took a break, went to the alley behind the bar, which was shared with an office building, and listened to the recording of his voice.

I sat on the side of the office building's concrete entry and called him. He answered. He told me he was glad I got his number and called him. He told me his wife found my address on the internet. He asked me how I was doing. I gave him some updates. I went to school and finished. He told me that was great. I had been bartending. He told me he used to bartend himself. I was gay. He told me he had been around the block and was tolerant. I had a couple ex-boyfriends. He told me heartbreak was something he knew something about. My mom had early onset dementia. He told me he was very sorry to hear that. He told me I sounded mature. He mentioned I had blocked my step-mom and step-sisters on social media. He told me they wanted to keep those relationships alive, that it hurt them. He asked me to apologize to my step-mom and step-sisters. He asked me if that made sense. I told him it made sense that he was asking that. We scheduled a time to meet, late Sunday morning at a brunch restaurant four weeks from then.

The night before, I was up all night doing cocaine with my friend. I stayed over at his place. I did not sleep. A couple hours before I was supposed to meet my dad, lying awake on the couch, I got up, showered, and dressed. I walked west through Glendale, up Cherry Creek towards south of downtown.

I walked up the sidewalk on South Logan Street to the restaurant. My dad was standing outside with his hands in his pockets. He saw me. We walked towards each other and hugged. He told me our table was not ready yet. He asked me who I thought was more nervous, me or him. I told him I thought he was more nervous. I told him I was more heavy-hearted than nervous.

We were seated by the host at a two-person table in the center of a busy dining room. I ordered coffee and he ordered decaf. I asked him why he ordered decaf, and he told me he only drank one cup of caffeinated coffee a day, the rest decaf. There was a large, long table to my left with a family seated at it, celebrating a graduation. It was loud in the dining room, but my dad and I talked quietly.

He asked me some more about my mom. I told him more about what was going on with her, and he cried. He told me he and my mom were once in love, and that his mom died of a brain tumor when he was my age. He asked me about the bar, what sort of place it was. I told him it was a gay bar, a bear bar. He asked me what a bear was. I told him a bear was an older, full-figured, hairy man. I asked why my step-sister's wedding was called off. He told me it was because her fiancé was a drinker. He told me her fiancé did not have much of a soul.

After we ate and he paid the bill, I asked him if he wanted to walk around. He told me that sounded nice. We walked towards downtown. I brought up him asking me to apologize to my step-mom and step-sisters. He told me that was stupid and apologized. He told me he did not know where I was coming from. I went on and told him I blocked them on social media to protect my feelings, that the experiences I had when I was a child at his and my step-mom's house were hard, that I never felt welcome there. He told me he understood.

We kept walking. We were about to cross Speer Boulevard and enter lower downtown and southwest Capitol Hill. I told him about my failed romantic relationships. I told him both my ex-boyfriends made me feel like I was not good enough, but in different ways. They both broke up with me. He told me all the men in my life had left, including himself in that. He told me I was looking for relationships with men that reminded me of the feelings of the men in my life who left. He called it a compulsion pattern. He told me you can be aware of it, but it does not mean you can change it. He was a Licensed Clinical Social Worker. He worked with children. He told me when he was ten and his dad died, he blamed himself for it. He asked me if I was in therapy. I told him I had gone to a few appointments with people who took Medicaid.

We were walking north up Lincoln and about to pass the bar. I told him we were about to pass the bar. I did not want to pass the bar with him. He told me we did not have to if I did not want to. We turned and walked east through Capitol Hill. He asked me about going to school for writing, and what I was doing with my degree now that I was done. I told him I was a writer, that bartending gave me time to write, and that my first book came out this year. He asked me if he could read it. I told him I used a pen name and nobody in my family could read it unless they sleuthed it, which I would appreciate if they did not do that. He told me one of my step-sisters was a writer, too.

We turned and walked north through Capitol Hill, not far from my ex-boyfriend's apartment. I told him there was a park, Washington park, where we could sit down. He was breathing hard and sweating. He told me he could not move around like he used to. Across the street from the park, I told him I imagined he felt a lot of guilt. I told him it was okay. I told him I was okay. It was fine. I was fine. He told me he did feel guilt. He thanked me for saying that.

We crossed the street and sat in the park under the shade of a large tree. People were playing soccer. He told me stories about my relatives on his side of the family. We talked about the state of the world. He told me stories about sports and asked if I still played. I told him I exercised, but did not play any organized sports.

He looked at his phone and told me he had to get going. He called his wife and told her he would be back soon. He handed the phone to me so I could talk to her. I told her maybe I could visit them on the East Coast sometime. She told me that was big, and would take planning. I told her goodbye. I handed the phone back and he asked me if that was awkward, then apologized.

He asked me where we were and I told him the cross streets. I asked him if he had a car service application on his phone. He told me he did not, but could call a cab. He asked me how I was getting home. I told him I was taking the bus, that it picked up by the park. He called a cab. We waited and talked some more. The cab arrived. I told him I loved him. He told me he loved me. We hugged. He got in the cab and left. I waited for the bus.

A PICK-UP ARTIST IN THE ANIMAL KINGDOM

I finished editing a poem and left Diane's house, in Edgerton, for RUFF'S, in Madison, a twenty-five minute drive, in her car. It had a hole in the front bumper, a box of Duraflame logs in the backseat. It was the end of January, a Friday. I had moved back to the area after eight years and landed with Diane, my old friend's mom. I tended bar at RUFF'S in my earlier twenties, which were about to be over in the summer. My last stint at the bar did not end well. But I was older, and a much better bartender now. I worked at a high-volume, destination bear bar when I was in Denver, from where I had just moved a couple weeks ago, to be closer to my mom, who was sick. The bar was called Denver Honey. Its logo was an emoji-esque bear head set on top of a paw with golden honey dripping from it. Yum! Woof! Arf! Grr! Bears, otters, wolves, pups and their handlers, leather daddies and their boys, and just plain gay guys—I had mingled with and served them all. I knew how to do it. There was nothing to it. I was a sometimes pleasant, sometimes catty robot behind the bar. My wit was honed. My honey was sweet. My body was covered in psoriasis lesions. A stress outbreak I was trying to get under control. I did not want to work in a gay bar again after leaving Colorado, but I texted Gino once I got to Wisconsin, to see if he needed help, because I needed help myself. I was on the ever-present cusp of broke-a-tude. He did need help. Help was wanted. He had opportunities. I had a stellar letter of reference from the owner of Honey, describing my "fun quarky" sense of humor. I was not just funny: I was subatomically hilarious. I wished he had let me proofread his letter. That was something I did on the side for extra money. I would have done it for him for free, an errorless letter being in my interest. I appreciated the gesture, though. I was grateful. I had no complaints. None.

Gino and I met over coffee across the street from RUFF'S, before he opened the bar. He had started tending bar three happy hours a week, he said, because it let him "keep track of things." He asked me what had changed since I last worked for him. I told him I had changed. I grew up. I was no longer resistant to posting about my shifts on Facebook, a sure sign of adulthood, which had always seemed to evade me in the past. He offered me a job. He said I could have whatever I wanted. I would take on some shifts, yes. Yes, Gino, I will work for you again. He was an older, stocky, grey-haired man of Italian descent with a beard like a genie's. He was somebody's type. Somebody I never wanted to meet! There goes that wit of mine. Up the river like a spawning salmon toward a bear. Grr! Chomp!

I parked on the street outside RUFF'S three minutes before 5, the start of my re-training shift, and dropped some quarters in the meter. I looked good. I had gotten a fade the other day to look the part. This otter's noggin was fresh, with minimal dandruff, thanks to some topical corticosteroids. I strode into the bar like I did not own the place. Gino greeted me.

"Did you not get a RUFF'S shirt?"

"Oh, I mean, yeah. You gave me one. It's in the rotation. Did you want me to wear it?"

"Well, yeah! Get one from downstairs. They're in the crates." Gino shook his head and rolled his eyes, looking to the full bar of patrons. What he was looking for in them, I knew not. Affirmation of his impatience and disdain for me, maybe. Just a guess.

"Okay, cool. Thanks, sorry. Won't happen again, sir. I'm just gonna hang my coat up."

"This is why you show up fifteen minutes before your shift."

"Oh, I just thought since it wasn't a shift change and I'm not relieving you—joining you rather—that I could show up when you told me to. I'm just gonna hang my coat up."

The back room was dark. I searched with my fingers for a switch.

"Why are you turning my bar lights down?"

"Oh, sorry, I can't find it."

He came over, head still shaking, and found the switch for me, one of about eight.

"It's this one here on the top left." He flipped it and nothing changed. "Or I guess the top right."

The room lit up and I hung my coat on a hook. I opened the downstairs door.

"Which shirt did I give you?"

"It was the Pride one. The Stonewall fiftieth. The ringer tee."

"Get a different one."

I descended to the basement and the smell hit my memory of it. Reunited at last. Oh, how I missed you so, moist concrete. I found a different shirt in my size and removed it from its plastic bag. I shed the one I was wearing, a shirt with an angry-looking, open-mouthed bear's face on the back. Roar! The basement's cool, wet air soothed the rashes on my back. I put on my RUFF'S shirt, which was different—so very different—and went back upstairs.

"You remember how all this works, right?"

Gino patiently and graciously reacquainted me with the touchscreen point-of-service system above the register, an older version of Aloha, which is what I had used at Honey, except at Honey, it was the newest version. It was better. Better, faster, and sleeker. The one I was looking at was the same one that was there eight years ago.

"Yeah, most of it."

"Clock in using the last four of your social."

I started tending bar. The robot, which had been dormant for a long three weeks, had been activated. Its hydraulics wheezed and creaked. I greeted the patrons, some of whom I knew from my previous tenure there.

"You still drink Miller Lite bottles and shots of Jameson?"

"I switched to rum and diet, but that's remarkable," said Dean.

Dean-o was always my favorite. In a violent clash between Gino and Dean-o, if I was the judge—and I was—Dean-o would be the victor.

"Bryan, you like gimlets, yeah?"

"I'll be damned."

"Hey, I don't have to remember much. What about you? I don't remember your name but you do Seagram's VO and diet, right?"

"Yes!"

"What's your name again?"

We shook hands. It seemed like people were happy to see me. They were happy to have me back. Those I didn't know, well, they would learn. I would teach them.

"You ready for another? What are you having?"

"He'll tell you when he's ready. He drinks paper planes. I'll show you how to make one when he needs one," said Gino, leaning into me and lowering his voice, "we don't want customers drinking too fast. We want them to stay as long as possible. Helps keep the atmosphere of the bar."

The atmosphere, of course. What was I thinking? I knew how to make a paper plane like the patron's, which was almost empty, but I decided against mentioning it. I would not want to bristle any fur. Arf!

I went to give another patron a refill. He had a tall glass, so I made him a double.

"He drinks single talls," said Gino.

"Oh, my bad."

"Yeah, we don't want customers to get too drunk too fast. We want them to stay."

We wanted them to stay, but did I want to stay?

"Sorry."

I brought the patron his drink, a whiskey diet.

"Let's talk about these pants," he said, "they're a little baggy. We need to get you in something tighter. We need to get that shirt off."

"What, you don't like these joggers?" I spun around like a model, putting my hands on my hips and thrusting my elbows forward while sucking in my cheeks and making a pouty face.

"I'm just giving you a hard time." He laughed.

"Hey," I got closer to him, lowering my voice and tenderly touching his elbow, "I'd take my shirt off, but—"

"I need you to get some ice from downstairs and refill the cherries," said Gino.

"—Tell you about it later."

"What happened to the ice scoop?" said Gino.

71

"Oh, I left it in the well. Was that wrong?"

"Now you have to wash it. I don't know how you did things in Denver . . ."

I washed the ice scoop, which had been made suddenly filthy by sitting in the very ice it was used to scoop. I grabbed the ice buckets from their hooks in the back. I went downstairs and filled them up, not feeling, at this point, in a rush to return. I filled up the ice wells. I looked for a glove to grab the cherries, but could not find one. This robot did not remember everything, after all.

"Hey, Gino," I apprehensively placed my hand on his back as he chatted with a patron, "sorry, where are the gloves?"

"Top of the stairs."

I put on a glove and headed to the cooler in the back, fished out a handful of cherries.

"Make sure to put the juice in there, too."

I flinched and almost knocked over the large container of cherries floating in their "juice." Gino was behind me, standing in the doorway of the cooler. The gay Italian genie had appeared.

"Yessir."

You will get your juice, Gino Bianchi. Worry not, for I am your juice man. I am the deity of nectar. The otter of your loins. Mwah! I returned to the bar with the cherries, and the goddamn juice.

"Want another?"

I knew Dean-o did. He always did, until he did not. I made a single tall rum and diet.

"He drinks doubles," Gino said, "just assume our customers want doubles. We make more money that way."

I had done just that, just before, and was corrected for doing so. Which was it, singles or doubles? I was confused. I was so confused, in fact, that I was beginning to get upset.

"Here you go, Dean-o."

"Do you want a shot with me? Gino, can he have a shot?"

"No, he's training. He's on probation."

Jail sounded better. Lock me up, daddy bear. Slam the door. Slide me my food and leave me alone. I refilled another patron's drink, the one who drank single talls.

"That's a double," Gino said, "you poured him a double."

"Oh, I thought I poured him a single."

"No, you poured him a double."

"Very well."

All the liquor bottle nozzles had small weights inside them. Perfect pours. Exact pours. Nothing extra. You get what you pay for and nothing more. I remembered this from when I last worked there. Somehow, now, I hated it more.

"Dan-o is coming in, remember what he drinks?" said Gino.

"Miller Lite bottles and Jager bombs, right?"

"That's right. If you have it ready for him, he'll be impressed."

The Jagermeister was in a machine that refrigerated it close to freezing, with a convenient spout mounted on the front.

"Is the handle stuck?"

"You have to do it sideways."

"Oh, weird."

"Fill it to that line and fill the Red Bull to an inch below the rim."

"You got it." I tilted the spout handle sideways.

"Whoa!"

I let go of the handle. "What's up?"

"Oh, that's fine."

I brought Dan-o his beer and bomb.

"Oh, you remembered! I love you." He held my hand.

Gino, Dean-o, and Dan-o. I thought about it. Dan-o was Curly and Dean-o was Larry. Gino, without a doubt, was Moe.

Louis, the bar manager and a former coworker of mine, showed up to relieve Gino, who relieved himself at 7, two hours before the other bartenders. Gino was a man who made his own rules, as well as everybody else's. I gave Louis a hug. It was really good to see him.

I went to the bathroom, and when I returned, Gino was laughing, but not smiling. He was shaking his head.

"Hey, would you mind not leaving the Red Bull cans in front of the door of the cooler, please, so I don't knock them on the floor and make a mess?" Gino looked at Dan-o knowingly, half-laughing, half-scoffing. Dan-o looked at me and frowned. He was on my side, but he was also in Gino's bar. RUFF'S.

I made a mistake. I had an accident. Whoops. I felt terrible about it. Nevermind that Gino did not see the can there, in front of the cooler door, before he opened it. It was my fault, and my fault alone. Nobody else was responsible for what had happened. Nobody but me.

"Clean this up. You can use a rag from the back. Don't use a white one."

I went to the back and Louis was there. I asked him where the rags were. He showed me. I grabbed a blue one, returned to the scene of the crime, and cleaned it.

"Which rag did you use?"

I showed it to Gino.

"Okay, that's fine."

I was glad it was fine. I just wanted everything to be fine. Gino clocked himself out and Louis took over.

"I'll have a tall Dewar's and soda with a single shot in it," said Gino.

I made the boss his drink and he sat next to Dan-o. Another patron asked for a refill. I turned to Gino.

"Double, right?" I smirked, knowing how much I wanted to rip his beard out of his face with my fist. Grant me this final wish, my genie, so you may return to your lamp and be buried deep in Sicilian sands. Gino rolled his eyes. I wanted a cigarette, a habit I picked up over Pride in Denver, but I knew better than to do it while my overlord was present.

Gino finally left. The last hour or so of my shift with Louis went by smoothly. He and I worked well together. It was fun. At 9, my relief showed up. He was someone I had never seen before. He was a balding ginger bear with glasses and a thick ass. The rare ginger bear, a weakness of mine. A thick ass, also a weakness. I was having a moment of frailty. He was adorable. I was smiling uncontainably.

"I don't think I've ever seen you before in my life," I said, "what's your name?"

"Tim. It's nice to meet you."

"It's nice to meet you, Tim."

I clocked out and sat at the bar, and Tim talked to me. We talked for five minutes straight. That is a long time to talk to a bartender. I was making him laugh. I could tell he was smart. I told him I was an artist, a writer. He told me he was a local politician. I told him that was really cool, and I admired people who could do that, because I could never. I told him I was looking for a place in Madison, and he told me he was connected to cheap housing resources, and could help me. I told him that would be great. I went outside and had a cigarette. I texted Diane.

"I don't want to work here."

When I returned, Tim was not wearing his shirt anymore. I was smiling. He was smiling. Smiles, smiles, smiles. I closed my eyes and looked down shyly, shaking my head.

"I have to go now."

I did not have to go. I did not want to. I wanted to talk to Tim. I wanted to look at him. I wanted to make him laugh. I should have left, though, and I did. Diane texted me earlier that it was snowing between Madison and Edgerton.

It was Saturday. I had the weekend off. My next shift was Monday. More re-training with Gino. I texted him.

"Hi Gino, yesterday was good. Thanks for everything. I can't make it to the event tonight. I know you wanted me there. Bummer. I was going to ask you for Tim's phone number. He said he was going to help me find a place in Madison. I'm going to create a Facebook profile tomorrow, by the way, to promote my resurgent role at the bar."

He texted me Tim's phone number. I texted Tim.

"Hi Tim, this is Ben, your new coworker at the bar. It was great to meet you yesterday. I wanted to reach out, because you mentioned that, when the time comes for me to leave the boonies, you could direct me to some channels/resources re: housing in Madison. Also we should hang out, if you'd like. You seem awesome."

"Thanks! Working right now. Gino mentioned he was giving you my number. I did a couple reach-outs since Gino told me a couple hours ago. If you're looking for a place right away, I know one person in town who has an efficiency available now through May 31st for 540. It's the off season, so a sublet is probably your best bet since it's almost impossible to get leases that start now."

"That's a good price. I'll need to work for a few weeks first. But something like that would be perfect. Thanks a lot!"

"Yeah I'll keep asking around too so let me know when you're closer to needing a place. We should totally hang out sometime too btw :)"

"That is what is up."

It was an hour before my shift on Monday, and I was dreading it. I had created a Facebook page on Sunday, and the bar friends rolled in. I was up to almost one-hundred already. I texted Gino.

"Gino, I hate to tell you this, but I can't work for RUFF'S, effective immediately. I'm not coming in this afternoon, or ever again, at least as a bartender (provided I'm not now 86'd for such a sudden departure). I've thought about it a great deal, and I know it's the right choice for me. I also know you will be completely fine without me. You've been fine and great for 14 years. I know such short notice is shitty, and I feel terrible about it. But I seriously cannot go through with this. I want to thank you so much for giving me the opportunity to return, but I especially want to extend my gratitude to you for talking to me about what's happening to my mom and everyone around her because of what's happening to her. I hope you're not *too* pissed off about this. It has to suck. I'm sorry. All Best."

"Ummmmm . . . ok! Did something happen to create such a major departure from where you were last week!?"

"What happened, happened within me. I love everyone at the bar. I just can't work there."

"Well ok then."

I deleted my Facebook. Tim texted me.

"What happened! No more RUFF'S?"

"No more RUFF'S. It was both a very hard and very easy decision to make. I'm going to tell you some things in confidence here, because I instantly felt a trust with you after meeting you. All it took was 3 hours behind the bar with Gino to know I didn't want to do it. But more, to ever work in a gay bar again. It's all I've done, pretty much. Right off the bat, he was on top of me and up my ass with criticisms, demeaning me in front of a full bar of patrons. He said I was late. I was on time. I make it a rule to show up early for shift changes, but I wasn't taking over for anyone. I was joining Gino to 're-train.' He criticized me for not wearing a RUFF'S shirt, as if one needs a uniform for that job. I told him it was in the rotation, that I just didn't wear it *that day*. He was not okay with that. It reminded me of everything that made working for him miserable. A customer nearly tried to suck my face off when he said goodbye. Another one, while I was smoking outside, tried the same. I was a very successful bartender in Denver. One of the most. I was beloved there. If you went there with me, and we went to a bar, you would understand and know this. It seemed Gino's primary goal on Friday was to humiliate me and put me in my place as his subordinate. But we all know who really makes bars run. It's the managers and bartenders and bar-backs and door-persons. The owner's authority is general, and s/he should entrust a dedicated staff with the details. But he's a micro-manager. He wouldn't let me breathe. He even said, when I left an ice scoop in the bin (an entirely normal and non-health-code-violation act), 'I don't know how you did things in Denver . . .' I'd have taken it jocularly with anyone else, but it struck me as definitely mean-spirited and cruel. It re-dawned on me just how humorless, grave, and arrogant he is at what he does. I don't like him, as a human being. Please don't share what I'm saying with anyone. Maybe you have a different relationship with him. He treated me like shit. I'm trying to move forward in my life. I just finished my second book the other day and I'm waiting to hear back from publishers. I have a skill-set and resume that exceeds any bar. I don't need it. I know the short notice was shitty, but he and everyone else there will be fine, barring minor scheduling inconveniences. I have other opportunities. Mickey's Tavern, for instance. Also I was really hoping I wouldn't develop a crush on any of my coworkers, and that happened last Friday when I met you, to both my delight and somewhat chagrin. I bet you saw right through me. I feel like I was pretty transparent. I'm not good at hiding in that way, or 'playing it cool.' You seem so wonderful to me, and I hope we can stay in touch, and even get together sometime. I'm not saying everyone should hate Gino or anything, but I can't permit myself to work for him. What can I say, my tolerance for him is thin, and I, a grown man, refuse to be treated like a child by another grown man. Also, 8 years ago he fired me by taking me off the schedule without any notice. I was 22. It cast me into hardship. So I don't have much sympathy for making the life he chose for himself any harder. I wasn't fired this time. Pettiness plays rough."

"You're not the only person to say that stuff about Gino. I have a good relationship with him but I also mostly started working again there just because he was low on staff. I know a lot of other folks have had different experiences. The RUFF'S community can be a bit much too sometimes. I did pick up on the other thing Friday though. You were a bit obvious ;). Shame too about RUFF'S. I was looking forward to running into you tonight. Celebrating my b-day :)."

"We can have a late celebration. Gino and I are done, but I have an intuition that you and I are not. Happy Birthday, Tim. You were the best thing about last Friday for me, by far."

"Thanks it's tomorrow, but I have to do forum prep and then stream a school board forum tomorrow so today is the day for celebrating :)."

"I feel it might be in bad taste for me to show up to RUFF'S tonight."

"Just a bit, it won't do you and Gino any good. He's good at reestablishing that customer-owner relationship though so don't bar yourself from coming back."

"I want to lay low anyhow. But I also want to go on a date with you, if you'll allow it. Even just to get to know each other more."

"If I'll allow it huh?"

"I mean. I'm just trying to be respectful. You're a politician. Your wheelhouse is the concealment of emotions in the service of policy and representation. I'm an artist. I do the opposite of that. Hope you find that cute."

"I'd love to go out sometime. What's your schedule like?"

"(Checks calendar) wide open."

"What are you up to Wednesday?"

"(Checks calendar once more) nothing."

"Care to grab a drink? Since you mentioned Mickey's already how about there?"

"It's my favorite place in town."

"I like it because it's close to where I live so I can walk there :)."

It is Tuesday afternoon, Gino. Tomorrow, I am going on a date with one of your bartenders. I am pretty into him. He seems pretty into me, too. Did you know he has a pet parrot? He is a Congo African Grey. They both have the same life expectancy. Wild. I am looking forward to meeting him. Maybe Tim and I will come into your bar together, once you have cooled off. Are parrots allowed? I am not in any rush. You will not be able to do anything about it, anyway, when it happens. I am proud of myself, Gino, for standing up for myself. I hope you are proud, too. I have had enough of the animal kingdom. I bet Tim found that attractive. Woof!

EPILOGUE

DOUBT DOUBT

You're not confident enough in your writing. Not like you should be. It almost makes me angry in an incredulous way. Really, it's like you're not confident that your life is interesting, on its own, as writing. Your life is imminently interesting, fascinating on its own. Just on its own. It doesn't have to be adorned with anything to make it amazing, because it already wholly is. I'm saying this because I've had this problem myself. I'm still constantly having it and fighting it. The solution that we create to this problem that doesn't exist is we try to make our lives in our writing more interesting with other things, because we feel like our lives are not enough. But they are enough. They don't need extra literary things to make them enough. In fact, the added, self-conscious work detracts from what makes our lives so interesting. We can't ever see it ourselves, because we're with ourselves all the time and can't get away. Maybe crowding our work with superfluous stuff to make what is already incredible and vivid and real more interesting is our attempt to get away from our uninteresting lives. But the entire point of this in the first place, the reason why I started at least, was to figure things out. Go more into yourself. Fully. We should become more of ourselves by writing, not less. When writing, it's not about thinking of something literary to write to make your life interesting. It's not thinking of what to write, it's remembering the thing itself better, harder, with the full force of your mind and heart behind it. Just knowing you're a good, worthwhile person. Being merciless with who you were. Because it's who you were, not who you are. Because you're a human being and you can change yourself. You've changed before and you'll do it again. I'm trying to change myself right now. I didn't write regularly for like a year. Who cares? That's who I was. Now, I'm a guy who writes something every day, because I know if I just do what I'm talking about, it will be enough. Enough to sustain me, fuck everybody else. They're lucky to know even a small part of my life. It doesn't need work. It needs less work. I need to tell myself this stuff all the time if I expect to muster the will to write. I have to constantly remind myself to stop doubting that my life is interesting and to step back and instead doubt the thing that is doubting that my life is interesting. Doubt that doubt. The mechanism of doubt. That doubt isn't you: it's everybody else. It's your distorted perception of everybody else, which we're always dealing with and having to let dismantle itself under the pressure of our frank gazes. It's about the quality and astuteness and unflinchingness of your observation of your life.

ACKNOWLEDGMENTS

Grateful acknowledgment is made to the editors of the publications in which the poems and prose in this book originally appeared (some in different form and under different titles):

BULL: Men's Fiction: "Denver, Colorado"; *Gay Death Trance*: "SLAB," "SLAB VII"; *Hobart*: "SLAB II"; *Muumuu House*: "A Pick-Up Artist in the Animal Kingdom"; *The Nervous Breakdown*: "Customer"; *New York Tyrant Magazine*: "The Gibson Damnation Resurfaces," "SLAB III," "Your First Ex-Boyfriend"; *The White Elephant*: "SLAB IV/V/VI"; *Young Magazine*: "Daddy State of Mind"

With gratitude to Sam Pink, Joey Russo, Patrick Welsh, Bill Martin, James Long, Diane Elver, Sean Kilpatrick, Tao Lin, Blake Butler, Nate Lippens, Junior Burke, Bhanu Kapil, Ben Webb, Giacomo Pope, Cowboy Roland, Jordan Castro, Giancarlo DiTrapano, Marston Hefner, Joey Grantham, Scorpio the Hierophant, "Dr. Dr." Jordan Bradford, Keith Jones, Robbie McMath, Joe Meyer, Cameron Daniel, Seth Kaplan, Tyler Sankey, Jorge Olguin, John Swayze, Rich Illgen, Chris Newell, Dutch Confetti, Steve Anderson, Will Ruarke, Chris Hostetter, Ken Maglasang, Randy Minten, DJ Zac Reclipze, Bradford West, DJ Craig C, Andrew Glardon, Draven Gonzales, Chad Wise, Jack Herrick, Scotty Pouland, Mattsicle, Brian Numbers, Mike Bortnowski, Chris Walkie, Jacob Leavitt, Derek Miller, Jesse Chavez-Van De Hey, Alex Delgado, Thera Marshall, Denver Health, Truvada, Gonorrhea, Ceftriaxone, Chlamydia, Azithromycin, and the cocaine dealers of Denver, Colorado.

—— ABOUT THE AUTHOR ——

Big Bruiser Dope Boy is the author of *Foghorn Leghorn* and *Your First Real Boyfriend & Other Poems*. He is the founder/editor of *Gay Death Trance*. He lives in Wisconsin, thank God.

11:11 Press is an American independent literary
publisher based in Minneapolis, MN.
Founded in 2018, 11:11 publishes innovative
literature of all forms and varieties. We believe
in the freedom of artistic expression, the
realization of creative potential, and the
transcendental power of stories.

CPSIA information can be obtained
at www.ICGtesting.com
Printed in the USA
FSHW010630090420
68993FS

9 781948 687225